Who is Holly?

I Talk You Talk Press

CONTENTS

1. THE DRESS

"What a beautiful dress!" said Glenda.

Jed was surprised. He looked at Glenda. "The dress?"

Glenda's face became pink.

"Sorry!" she said. "But I have never seen such a lovely dress."

The woman was young. She was lying face down. Her dress was long and strapless. It had a wide skirt. The skirt was spread out. She looked like a sleeping princess. But she was in a dark, narrow street behind a row of townhouses. And she was dead.

Jed and Glenda are detectives. They work in the Boston Police Department. They are partners. Glenda is 40 years old. She is a tall strong woman with short red hair. Jed is 35. He is shorter than Glenda. He thinks Glenda is very tough. He thinks she is stronger than him. She always wears jeans and T-shirts. So Jed was surprised when Glenda talked about the dress.

Jed and Glenda watched the medical and technical staff while they worked. It was a strange scene. The technicians had set up bright lights so they could see well. After a few minutes, one of the policemen walked over to them. Jed knew him. His name was Pete.

"Who found her?" asked Glenda.

"I did," answered Pete. "I was driving down the main road, when I saw something on the ground in this street. I stopped and came to look."

"Does the doctor know when she died?" Glenda asked.

"He's not sure. But he thinks about ten thirty pm," said Pete. "It's midnight now, so she died about one and a half hours ago. He says someone hit her on the back of her head. He will make a report

1

tomorrow."

"Do you know who she is?" asked Jed.

"Yes. We couldn't find a handbag, or any ID. But we took a picture of her. We talked to all the people in the townhouses. A young woman, called Linda Stein knew the woman in the picture. She said the dead woman was Holly Warburton. They were housemates."

"We should go and talk to her," said Glenda.

"Yes," said Jed. "Which townhouse is it, Pete?"

"Number fourteen," said Pete. "That is the back door over there." He pointed to one of the doors in the brick wall along one side of the street. "But it is easier to go to the front door in the next street. A policewoman is there."

"OK, Pete," said Jed. "Thanks."

Jed and Glenda walked to the next street. It was wider. The town houses looked expensive. Number 14 was in the middle of the row. The lights were on in the downstairs rooms.

Jed and Glenda walked up to the door and rang the bell. A young policewoman answered the door.

"We've come to talk to Linda Stein," said Glenda.

"Sure," said the policewoman. "I don't think we met before. I'm Sandra. Come in. She is very upset, but I think she can talk to you."

2. LINDA

Glenda and Jed walked into the townhouse.

"She's in here," said Sandra. She walked through the entrance hallway, and turned right into a living room. Glenda and Jed followed her.

Jed looked around the room. It was very bright and warm. There were two small leather sofas, bookcases and tables in light coloured wood, and some very colourful modern art on the walls.

The young woman sitting on one of the sofas was wrapped in a blanket. She was holding a cup in both hands. Her face was white, and her eyes were red from crying. There was a box of tissues on the side table next to the sofa.

"These detectives have come to talk to you," said Sandra. "Would you like another cup of tea?"

The young woman shook her head. "No, thank you," she answered.

Glenda walked across the room and sat on the sofa next to the young woman.

Jed sat down on the other sofa. Sandra stood by the door.

"I know you are very tired and upset," said Glenda quietly. "I am sorry to ask you questions now, but we need your help."

"The young woman tried to smile. "OK."

"What is your name?"

"I'm Linda Stein. I live…" Linda stopped. Then she tried to speak again. "I lived here with Holly…" Linda started to cry. "The policeman showed me a photograph! It was Holly! The policeman said she was dead! I don't understand!"

"It's OK," said Glenda. "Of course you don't understand. We don't understand either. But please help us. Please tell us everything. How did you meet Holly?"

Linda drank some tea and put the cup on the side table. She took a deep breath.

"Yes. Sorry. I will try," she said. "I am a student at Lincornvale College. I am a sophomore. I come from New Jersey. When I came to Boston last year to go to college, I lived with my uncle. My family doesn't have much money, and it was cheaper than living in the dormitory. Then my uncle got transferred to California. I had nowhere to live. Holly was in my history class. I didn't know her well. But she heard I was looking for somewhere to live. She asked me to be her housemate. She said she didn't want to live alone. I was so happy. The rent is very low and it is a beautiful house."

Jed was surprised. "This is a very expensive neighbourhood. Why is the rent low?"

Linda nodded. "I thought it was strange, but Holly said her aunt owned the house. She said her aunt was rich, and didn't want a lot of money. I thought I was very lucky."

"Did you like living with Holly?" asked Glenda.

"Oh, yes! Holly was a very nice person. We were good friends, and we never had any problems."

"Tell me about today," said Glenda. "When did you see Holly?"

"I saw her this morning. We ate breakfast together, and walked to college. She had a history class and I had a French class. I didn't see her again. I can't believe she's dead!" Linda started to cry again.

"You didn't see her again?" asked Jed. "Was that normal?"

"Yes. We were good friends, but we didn't do everything together. And this year we have different classes. I have a job in a convenience store after school. When I got home about nine o'clock, she wasn't here."

"Did she tell you she was going out? Did she say where she was going?" asked Jed.

"No," answered Linda. "She didn't say anything. We were good friends. Holly was a lovely person. She was very kind and friendly, but she was private too. She never asked me what I was doing. And I never asked her. Sometimes we went to the movies, or to student parties, or to basketball games together. But she often went out and didn't say where she was going, or who she was going with."

Glenda showed Linda a photograph of Holly lying on the ground.

"I'm sorry Linda, but I have to ask you about this dress. It is the kind of dress young women wear to proms or formal dinners or parties. Are you sure Holly didn't say where she was going tonight? I am sure she would tell you if she was going to an important event."

Linda shook her head.

"No. She didn't say anything about a big event, and I have never seen that dress before. Holly had nice clothes, but I never saw her wear anything so formal or expensive."

"What about her family?" asked Jed. "Did you meet them? Did Holly talk about them?"

"Holly said her family lived in upstate New York. She never talked about them."

"And how about a boyfriend?" asked Glenda. "Did Holly have a boyfriend?"

"Oh, yes. His name is Raymond Kim. He is on the basketball team."

"Where does he live?"

"He lives in one of the dormitories," said Linda.

"Linda. I'm sorry. But can you tell us what you did after you got home at nine o'clock?" asked Glenda.

"I made a sandwich and some cocoa. Then I went to my room. I am studying French, but I am not good at speaking it. I have online conversation practice every Thursday with a native speaker. That was from nine thirty to ten thirty. Then I did research online for a report. I was still working on my computer when the police rang the doorbell."

Jed stood up.

"Linda. We will go and look in Holly's room. We want to look in your room too. Is that OK?"

"Sure," answered Linda.

Glenda stood up too.

"Stay here with Sandra. We will try to be quick. Where is your room?"

"If you walk straight through the entrance hallway towards the back of the house, my room is on the right, behind this room. It's next to the downstairs bathroom. Holly's room is upstairs."

Glenda and Jed went to Linda's room. It looked very normal. Jed looked at her laptop computer. It was still turned on. He looked at the browser.

"Someone was using this computer from about nine thirty. Linda's Skype account is still open. She was talking to someone for sixty-five minutes. I think her story is true."

"Let's go and look at Holly's room then," said Glenda. They walked back to the entrance hall and climbed the stairs. There were two doors at the top of the stairs. Jed opened one of the doors. They looked into an empty room.

"A bedroom, I guess," said Glenda. "But never used."

Jed turned to the other door. "So this must be Holly's room," he said. He tried to open it, but it was locked.

"That's strange," said Glenda. "Why did Holly lock her door? Can we break the door down?"

"I don't want to do that," answered Jed. He took out his phone and called Pete.

"Are you still out on the street?" he asked.

"The medical staff and technicians have just finished. They are taking the body away now."

"I know you didn't find a handbag, Pete. But did you find any keys?"

"Yes. The doctor gave them to me just now. She had a chain around her waist under the dress. It has two keys on it."

"Can you bring them to us?" asked Jed. "And could you please bring some gloves and evidence bags too? I left mine in the car."

"They found some keys. Pete will bring them to us," Jed told Glenda.

They waited outside Holly's room. They heard the doorbell ring and heard Sandra talking to Pete. Then Sandra came up the stairs with gloves and big evidence bags. She gave them to Jed. She gave a small plastic bag to Glenda. The keys were inside. Glenda and Jed put on gloves and Glenda took the keys out of the bag.

"This one looks like a house key," she said. "So I guess this smaller one is the key to this room."

She put the smaller key in the lock and unlocked the door.

3. HOLLY'S ROOM

Jed and Glenda walked in and looked around. It was a large room but it looked very empty. There was a narrow bed with a white cover in one corner. A small desk with a laptop computer was under the window that looked out over the street. On another wall were closet doors and a door to a small bathroom.

"We'll look quickly," said Glenda. "Tomorrow a team can come and search properly."

Jed looked at the desk, and Glenda looked through the drawers and closet.

"There is something strange about this room," said Glenda.

"What is strange?" asked Jed.

"It's very clean and tidy. But it's like a hotel room." answered Glenda. "There are no photos or pictures on the wall. I wonder about her clothes." Glenda opened the closet door and looked at the clothes inside. "Come and look at this!" she said to Jed.

Glenda showed Jed the clothes inside the closet.

"This is like two people," she said. "These clothes here, the jackets and jeans and short skirts, are student clothes. They are very nice, but not expensive. But then at this end of the closet there are suits and dresses. Very expensive designer labels. And they are not the clothes a student wears. They are clothes for an older woman. Maybe a businesswoman. The shoes are the same." Glenda pointed at the shoe rack in the bottom of the closet.

There were running shoes, and ankle boots and pretty sandals. But there were also very high-heeled formal shoes.

"It doesn't make sense," said Glenda. "Some of the formal clothes are in dry cleaner's bags. The dates are from two or three years ago. Did you find any letters or photographs in the desk?"

"No," answered Jed. "Nothing." He went back to the desk. "There are some papers about the university and some notes for classes. I'll take the laptop. Maybe there will be emails on it."

"Here is a bag with books and other things. I guess this is the bag she takes to school. And here is her student ID," said Jed. He looked at the ID. "Holly Warburton aged twenty. And the photograph matches the photograph of the dead girl."

He looked in the drawers of the desk. He found a folder with Holly's college registration papers in it.

"There's a home address and the names of her parents here. I will call the police station and ask someone to contact them. It will be terrible news for them. Their daughter is dead."

He took out his phone and spoke to their boss. When he finished the call, he smiled at Glenda.

"The boss says we can go home. She will call the parents. She wants us to report to her early tomorrow morning."

Glenda and Jed put the laptop, the papers from the desk and Holly's school bag into big plastic bags, and took them downstairs. Pete was standing in the hallway talking to Sandra.

"Pete. Are you going back to the police station?" asked Jed.

"Yes. Do you want me to take those bags with me?"

"Yes, please," said Jed.

"OK," said Pete. "I'll leave them in the evidence room. You can get them tomorrow."

4. HOLLY'S PARENTS HEAR THE NEWS

The next morning, Glenda and Jed both went to work early. They wrote a report of everything they saw, and did, the night before. Then they went to their boss's office.

Their boss is Mercedes Costa. Glenda and Jed like her. She is a very cheerful person and she is very nice to all the people who work in her team. But that morning, Mercedes looked tired and overworked.

"Good morning, Boss," said Jed. "Do you want to hear our report now?"

"Yes. Come in and sit down."

Glenda and Jed told Mercedes about Holly, Linda, the townhouse and Holly's room.

"Has the doctor's report come in?" asked Glenda.

"Not yet," said Mercedes. "Maybe around lunchtime, the doctor will send it to us."

"How about the parents? Did you have a chance to talk to them?"

"Yes, I did. I called them last night. I told them their daughter was dead."

"When are they coming to Boston?" asked Jed. "We need to talk to them as soon as we can."

"They are not coming," said Mercedes. "It was very strange. I hate making phone calls to tell people such bad news. Sometimes I call the local police, and ask someone to go to the house to give bad news. But last night, it was very late. So I called."

"And?" Glenda was interested.

9

"They seemed shocked, but very calm. The father said, 'we will talk about it and call you in the morning'. He called me about ten minutes ago. He said they didn't think it was necessary to come to Boston. When we finish all our examinations and tests, he wants us to send her body to Rochester. He gave me the name of a funeral company there. He said to contact the funeral company, and the company would arrange everything. I think it is very strange."

"I think so too," said Jed. "The address for Holly's parents was in Plattsburgh. Rochester must be more than three hundred miles from Plattsburgh. Why are they using a funeral company in Rochester?"

"I don't know," said Mercedes. "Maybe they have family in Rochester. The parents' reaction seems very strange, but it is not our business. Our business is to find the killer. Did Holly have a boyfriend?"

"Yes," said Glenda. "Holly's housemate, Linda, said his name is Raymond Kim. We will go and talk to him this morning."

"Do you know about any other friends?" asked Mercedes.

"No. But we have Holly's laptop. Maybe there are emails. But I guess she has password protection on her laptop. I might need a computer expert to help get into her files," answered Jed.

Mercedes sighed. "Of course you can give the laptop to one of our computer experts. But it might take a long time to get any help. Everyone is so busy, and I have so many team members away with colds and influenza. I don't have any other detectives to help you. So there will only be you two working on this murder. Do the best you can."

"It's OK, Boss," said Glenda. "We understand. We will go to see the boyfriend now."

"Come and see me when you have some more information," said Mercedes. "Good luck."

Glenda and Jed went back to the main office. Jed got Holly's laptop from the evidence room. "I will try to open the files and the email account," he said. "Maybe I will be lucky."

Glenda called the university. The office at the university told Glenda the times and places of all Raymond Kim's classes and the number of his dormitory room. Glenda also got Raymond Kim's mobile phone number.

She went to Jed's desk. He was not happy.

"Of course there is a password and I can't get past it. Maybe we can guess her password."

"Maybe her boyfriend will have some ideas," answered Glenda. "Let's go and talk to him."

Jed and Glenda drove to Lincornvale College.

"Do we have Raymond Kim's cell phone number?" asked Jed.

"Yes," said Glenda. "But I don't want to call him. He might run away if we say the police want to talk to him. Let's try to find him first."

"Where shall we look?' asked Jed.

Glenda looked at her notes. "It is nine am now and his first class starts at ten. So why don't we try his dormitory room?"

Lincornvale College is a new campus. It has many modern buildings in a large green park. Glenda and Jed looked at the campus map, and found Raymond Kim's dormitory building. They drove to the dormitory and climbed the stairs to the third floor. Raymond Kim's room was 316. Glenda knocked on the door. No one answered. Jed knocked very hard on the door.

"This is the police!" he shouted. "We want to talk to Raymond Kim."

5. RAYMOND

Glenda and Jed waited. They could hear sounds inside the room. Then the door opened. A very tall African man, wearing only boxer shorts, stared at them.

"Are you the police?" he asked.

"Are you Raymond Kim?" asked Jed.

"No. Raymond is my roommate. I'm Viktor Okafor."

"Where is Raymond?" asked Glenda.

"He is probably in the gym," answered Viktor. "I should be there too, but I slept late. You woke me up."

"Sorry about that," said Glenda. "Do you know where Raymond was last night?"

"Yes. Of course," said Viktor. "We were playing a basketball game in Providence."

"What time did you get back?"

"We got back about eleven pm. We were excited, because we had a good win. So the team got together here in this room to celebrate. The rest of the team left about one am and Ray and I went to sleep."

"Thanks," said Glenda. She looked at her campus map. "Which gym does Raymond go to? I can see three on this map."

"It's the gym next to this dormitory," said Viktor. "Very convenient for us!"

Glenda and Jed walked down the stairs, and out into the cool autumn sunshine. Glenda looked at the time on the campus clock tower.

"We should hurry," she said. "He has a class at ten am. I don't want to miss him."

"He can't be the murderer," said Jed. "The doctor said Holly died about ten thirty pm."

"I know. But I hope he can tell us something about Holly. I think she was a very interesting young woman."

"Maybe he can help with the password to her computer," said Jed. "I want to look at Holly's files and emails."

They found Raymond in the gym changing room. He was dressed in jeans and a T-shirt. He was putting his basketball shoes into his locker.

"Are you Raymond Kim?" asked Glenda.

"That's right," said Raymond. He smiled. "What can I do for you?" Raymond was also very tall. He had a round happy face and a spiky hairstyle that made him look even taller.

"I'm Detective Glenda Durek from the Boston Police Department," said Glenda, showing Raymond her badge. "And this is Detective Jedburgh Smith."

Jed showed Raymond his badge. "We want to talk to you about Holly Warburton. Why don't we sit down for a few minutes?"

Jed pointed to the bench in the middle of the changing room.

Raymond looked at his mobile phone. "I have a class in twenty minutes."

"I know," said Glenda. "But this is important. If you answer our questions, it will not take a long time."

Raymond sat down. Jed sat down next to him and Glenda leaned against one of the locker doors facing Raymond.

"Where were you last night?" asked Jed.

"Why?" asked Raymond.

"Please, just answer my question," said Jed.

Raymond told them about the basketball game in Providence and the celebration party in the dormitory room. His story was the same as Viktor's.

Glenda looked at Jed. Jed nodded.

"I'm sorry to tell you that Holly Warburton was murdered last night," she said.

"Murdered!" shouted Raymond. "But why? Who?"

"We don't know," answered Glenda quietly. "We hope you can help us find the answers."

"Of course!" Raymond looked very shocked.

"Was Holly your girlfriend?" asked Glenda.

"Yes. Well, I called her my girlfriend," answered Raymond.

"What do you mean?" asked Jed. "Was she your girlfriend, or wasn't she?"

Raymond was embarrassed. "It's hard to explain."

"Please try," said Glenda.

"OK. Holly is… Holly was very pretty. All the guys liked her a lot. I asked her out on a date and she said 'yes'. I was very surprised. There are many guys on campus who are more handsome than me. I am shy, and I am always practising basketball. And I am on a scholarship. I don't have much money. I don't have a car. I don't know why she chose me," said Raymond.

"Maybe she liked you," said Glenda gently. "That's much more important than looks or money."

"Maybe." Raymond's face was red. "But you don't understand. We went on dates, but she wasn't like a real girlfriend. We started dating last year, but we never kissed. I never met her family. I wanted her to meet my family but she said 'no'. Do you know what I think?" Raymond spoke loudly.

"No, what do you think?" asked Jed.

"She was very pretty and everyone liked her. People always think that pretty girls have boyfriends. She wanted to have a boyfriend, so people wouldn't talk about her."

"But you knew her very well. You were good friends." Jed was puzzled.

"No. We went out on dates for almost a year, but I didn't know her well. She was like a stranger. She talked to everyone at parties. She smiled and laughed a lot. She was the perfect girlfriend in public, but she never told me anything about herself."

"So you don't know her computer password?" asked Jed.

"Of course not. I have to go now." Raymond stood up. "I will be late for class." He picked up his backpack and walked towards the door. He stopped and looked back at Glenda and Jed.

"She was a lovely girl, and I am very sorry she is dead. I want to help you, but I don't know anything."

6. HOLLY'S LIFE

Glenda and Jed drove back to the police station. They got coffees from the machine and sat down at Glenda's desk.

"We are not making progress," said Jed. "We know her housemate didn't kill her, and her boyfriend didn't kill her. That's all."

"We don't know where she went last night," said Glenda. "She was wearing a very beautiful and expensive dress, but we don't know who she met. We don't know anything about her friends. We didn't find a cell phone. She never told anyone about her family..."

"Hey! Stop!" laughed Jed. "You are making me depressed! Let's make a list of everything we want to know."

"Good idea," said Glenda. "So we need information on her credit cards, her bank account, and her phone. We need to get inside her computer..."

"I want to find out about this aunt who rented the townhouse to Holly and Linda so cheaply," said Jed.

Mercedes came up to Glenda's desk. "Are you making progress?" she asked.

"Not really. We talked to the boyfriend. He has a whole basketball team as an alibi. He didn't do it," answered Glenda.

"Have the technical investigation team searched Holly's room yet?" asked Jed.

"No. I'm sorry," said Mercedes. "They have a lot of people away sick. They have more urgent work. The room is all sealed up and they will start as soon as they can. Maybe tomorrow. But here is the

15

doctor's report."

She put the report on Glenda's desk and went back to her office.

Jed and Glenda read the doctor's report.

"The doctor made a mistake," said Jed. "Look, he wrote 'age approximately thirty years'."

"Well he's very busy. I guess he meant approximately twenty years," said Glenda.

"It says here that she was in good health." Glenda read more. "The test showed no signs of drugs. Someone hit her on the back of her head. She didn't fall. So it was murder, not an accident."

"We don't know where she went, but it must have been an expensive place," said Jed. "It says her last meal was oysters and lobster. And she had some wine – probably champagne."

"We could guess that from the dress she was wearing," said Glenda. She rubbed her eyes. "I feel tired. I don't know what to do next."

"We'll take the list to the data technicians. I know they are busy, but they can find out all the things we wrote on the list," said Jed. "I'll take the laptop computer too. I am sure they can break the password."

Jed and Glenda walked out of the main office and into a small room filled with computers and big screens. Normally, there were four or five people working there. Today there was only one; a small man wearing a baseball cap backwards and a medical mask.

"Hi Leonard," said Jed. "Where is everyone else?"

"Sick," answered Leonard from behind the mask. "Don't come close to me. Stay there by the door! I don't want to catch a cold or influenza. That's why I am wearing this mask."

"We are working on the murder of Holly Warburton," said Glenda. "We need your help."

"Everyone needs my help," shouted Leonard. "It is crazy. Everyone wants data and information, and I am the only one here!"

"We need to find out about Holly Warburton's life. We want to look at her email and computer files. Her computer is password protected. I can't get in," said Jed.

"And we need credit card records, phone records, bank records…. Everything on this list."

Glenda did not want to make Leonard angry. She put the list down on a table near the door. Jed put the computer next to it.

"Please try, Leonard," said Glenda. "I know you are busy, but this was a young girl. We want to find her killer."

"I'll try," said Leonard. "But it won't be today. Even if I work all night, I can't start on your questions until tomorrow."

"OK, Leonard," said Jed. "We understand. Please just do your best."

It was time for lunch, so Jed and Glenda went out to their favourite diner. Glenda ordered an omelette and Jed ordered his favourite Swiss cheese and mushroom burger. They didn't talk until they had finished their meals. They were both thinking about the murder of Holly Warburton.

When their coffees came, Jed said, "What do you want to do next? I haven't got any ideas. And we won't get any data from Leonard until tomorrow at the earliest."

Glenda stirred her coffee, and looked out the window of the diner.

"I think we should go and visit Holly's parents."

"In Plattsburgh?" Jed was surprised.

"Yes. There is something very strange about the parents and I want to meet them."

"OK. I guess we could drive there. It will take four or five hours. Let's ask the boss."

Mercedes said they could go to Plattsburgh.

"You are not making any progress, so I guess you should talk to the girl's parents. Make sure you send me reports. And be sure to call the local police. Tell them who you are, and why you are in their area."

Jed went to the door of the data technicians' room and asked Leonard to email any information he found. Leonard didn't answer, but Jed was sure he had heard him.

They took a car from the car pool and drove to Jed's apartment so he could pack some clothes for the trip. Then they drove to the huge house outside the city centre, where Glenda lives with her husband Phillip, and three dogs. Glenda's husband is much older than her. He is a retired lawyer. Jed sat in the kitchen and talked to Phillip, while Glenda packed a bag. It was almost 4:00 pm when they finally left the Boston area. They drove through Manchester, and across New Hampshire into Vermont. They finally crossed Lake Champlain and were in New York State.

"It's late," said Glenda. "How far to Plattsburgh from here?"

"About another hour," said Jed. "Maybe you can find a motel or cheap hotel on your phone. We won't arrive in Plattsburgh until after nine pm."

Glenda found a motel and reserved two rooms. By the time they checked in, it was very dark and the streets of Plattsburgh were almost empty. They found a Chinese restaurant and ate quickly.

"I'm so tired," said Jed when they got back to the motel. "See you around seven thirty in the morning. We can't go and visit Holly's parents before nine, so there is no need to hurry."

"OK," said Glenda. "I'll see you in the morning."

7. HOLLY'S PARENTS

The next morning Jed and Glenda ate breakfast in a diner across the road from the motel.

"I checked my emails this morning," said Jed. "There was nothing from Leonard, but Mercedes sent a message. Holly's body is being released today. The funeral company will collect her body from Boston, and take it to Rochester this evening."

"We should hurry then," said Glenda. "Her parents will be going to Rochester and we might miss them."

"But they know we are coming. Won't they wait until we get there?" asked Jed.

"I called the police here in Plattsburgh, and told them we were coming. But I didn't call the parents," answered Glenda.

"Why not?" asked Jed.

Glenda finished her eggs and bacon while she thought about it.

"I don't know. I have a feeling there is something strange about Holly and her parents. I don't want them to know we were coming. I want to surprise them."

"OK," said Jed. He finished his coffee and stood up. "Let's go."

Mr and Mrs Warburton lived in a pretty old house on a country road about five miles north of Plattsburgh. It was surrounded by farmland. There were no other houses nearby. Jed drove in the gate and parked near the front door. They walked up to the door and Glenda rang the bell.

A tall woman opened the door.

"Mrs Warburton?" asked Glenda. "Mrs Amabel Warburton?"

"Yes?" The woman seemed surprised to see them. She had blonde hair, and very pale blue eyes. She looked very tired and ill.

"We are sorry to disturb you. It must be a very difficult time for you," said Glenda. "I'm Detective Glenda Durek from the Boston Police Department, and this is Detective Jedburgh Smith."

They showed Mrs Warburton their badges.

"We have come to talk to you and your husband about your daughter, Holly," said Jed. "May we come in?"

"Oh, yes. I guess so," answered Mrs Warburton.

She stood back and Glenda and Jed walked into the front hallway. "My husband is out," said Mrs Warburton. "He has gone to the dentist and the supermarket. I don't know when he will come back."

Glenda could see a living room through an open door.

"Shall we go and sit down?" she asked Mrs Warburton.

"OK. Would you like some coffee?"

Jed and Glenda sat down in the living room. Mrs Warburton followed them and then went through a door at the back of the living room. Soon they heard the sound of a coffee grinder. Mrs Warburton came back and sat down.

"Coffee will be ready soon," she said.

"First, Mrs Warburton, we are very sorry for your loss," said Glenda. "It must be very difficult for you. But we want to find out who did this terrible thing to your daughter. I hope you will help us."

Mrs Warburton looked surprised. "No. I mean yes. But no, I don't know anything."

"When did you last see your daughter?" asked Jed.

"Not long ago," answered Mrs Warburton.

"A week ago? A month ago?"

"Longer than that," said Mrs Warburton. "She doesn't come here often, and we don't go to Boston."

"But she calls you or sends text messages?"

"I guess so. But I can't talk about it."

Mrs Warburton looked very upset. She stood up and went out the kitchen. Glenda and Jed could hear her preparing coffee.

Jed looked at Glenda. "She doesn't want to talk to us," he said very quietly. "I wonder why?"

Mrs Warburton came back with a tray of coffee. She looked much better. But as she leaned over towards Glenda to give her a coffee cup, Glenda smelt alcohol.

She was drinking in the kitchen at nine-thirty in the morning, thought Glenda. *She is very upset about her daughter's death. Or maybe there is something else.*

Jed was looking out the window. "You have a beautiful garden," he said.

"Yes," Mrs Warburton smiled. "It is my hobby. It takes a lot of time and energy, but I love it."

"Did Holly like gardening?" asked Glenda.

"She didn't like gardening, but she loved the flowers," said Mrs Warburton. "She always picked the best ones to give to her teacher. Of course that was my old garden. The one I had before."

Glenda was looking around the living room. There were many photographs of a blond-haired boy and girl.

"Is that Holly when she was young?" she asked.

"Yes. And that's our son Paul."

Glenda put down her coffee cup and stood up.

"Mrs Warburton? Could we take a look at Holly's room please? "

"OK." Mrs Warburton looked worried. "But I don't know why."

"Maybe we can find a clue to who killed her," answered Glenda.

"I'll go outside and wait for your husband," said Jed.

Glenda followed Mrs Warburton upstairs. Holly's room was at the front of the house overlooking the flower garden. Glenda looked around. There were stuffed toys and Teddy bears on the bed. The wallpaper was pink and white.

"It's a very pretty room," said Glenda.

"We decorated it for Holly when she was nine," said Mrs Warburton. "She loves pink."

Glenda looked at the books in the bookcase. She looked at the white table under the window. Everything in the room looked perfect. She looked in the closet. The closet was empty.

"Mrs Warburton...."

Just then, they heard a car drive off the road. Glenda and Mrs Warburton looked out the window.

"My husband is back," said Mrs Warburton.

A tall man with grey hair climbed out of a car. Jed was waiting by the garage. They watched as the two men spoke.

Mr Warburton seemed very angry. He waved his arms and spoke in a loud voice. Glenda could not hear what he was saying, but she thought, *There's something wrong. I think I will go downstairs and help Jed.*

"Shall we go downstairs now?" she asked Mrs Warburton. Mrs Warburton nodded and the two women walked downstairs and into the garden.

"Is everything OK, Jed?" asked Glenda.

"Mr Warburton is not happy," answered Jed.

"No. I am not happy!" shouted Mr Warburton. "I am very angry! Why did you come here? You will upset my wife! You have been inside the house! If I was here when you arrived, I would have told you to go away!"

"But Mr Warburton," Glenda was very surprised. "We are trying to find out who killed your daughter! Don't you want to help us?"

"I don't care! If you want to find out who killed her, look in Boston! Not here. Now go away."

"OK, Mr Warburton," said Jed. "But you will have to talk to us sometime."

Jed and Glenda got in the car and drove back into the town.

"We'll go and talk to the local police," said Glenda.

8. A SON BUT NO DAUGHTER

Jed parked outside the police station and they went in. They introduced themselves to the man at the front desk and showed their IDs.

"Welcome to small town America! I'm Denny Nowak. My boss told me you had called last night. Have you seen the family of the murdered woman?"

"Yes," said Glenda. "But they won't talk to us. We thought maybe you have some information about them."

"I don't know if we have any useful information. But come and talk to Captain Hollister."

Denny took Glenda and Jed into Captain Hollister's office.

"These are the Boston cops," said Denny. "They need some help."

Captain Hollister stood up from his desk and shook hands. "Welcome to Plattsburgh," he said. "Take a seat."

Glenda and Jed sat down, and Denny went back to the front desk.

"How can we help you?" asked Captain Hollister.

Jed told the captain the whole story.

"It's very strange," he finished. "The family seem shocked, but they don't seem sad. They didn't come to Boston. Their daughter's body is being taken to Rochester. The father told us to go away. Something is wrong."

"Maybe," said Captain Hollister. "I don't know anything about them, but I will ask my junior detective to get some information. Why don't you come back after lunch? Maybe we will have some data by then."

"Thank you very much," said Glenda. "We appreciate your help."

Glenda and Jed left the police station.

"Coffee?" asked Glenda.

"Can we go back to the motel?" said Jed. "I want to see if Leonard has found anything on Holly's computer."

There were no messages from Leonard. Glenda went to her own room and called her husband. They talked for a few minutes about the garden and the dogs. Then she lay down on her bed and fell asleep.

It was 12:30 when she woke up. Jed was knocking on the door. She went to the door and opened it.

"Why did you wake me up?" she asked. "I was having a beautiful dream!"

"Leonard sent a long email. You must read it!" Jed was excited.

Glenda went to the bathroom, and washed her face and hands. She felt much better. Jed put his computer on a small table and Glenda sat down to read Leonard's email.

Jed waited impatiently while Glenda was reading. When she finished, she stared at the computer screen.

"I don't understand," she said. "Leonard says that there are emails and files for two, or maybe three, different people on the computer. There are study notes and reports that seem to belong to Holly Warburton. A few emails that Holly Warburton received from her teachers and from friends. Of course there are her answers too. They are very normal."

"Yes," said Jed. "But then there are many files and business accounts and business emails that belong to someone called Cristina Martin. There are no personal emails for Cristina Martin. I called Leonard and talked to him.

"Leonard said he is still working on the files. But it seems Cristina Martin is a successful businesswoman in New York. She imports leather bags and shoes from Spain and sells them to boutique fashion shops. She also owns two apartment buildings in New York. Leonard checked on the townhouse in Boston where Holly was living with Linda Stein. That belongs to Cristina Martin too. The only thing is that all the Cristina Martin files and emails are old. They seem to stop about two years ago."

Glenda rubbed her eyes. "This makes my head hurt," she said. "Is

Cristina Martin Holly's aunt? Or did Holly Warburton have two lives? Maybe that is why she had two kinds of clothes. But what does Leonard mean about the third person?"

"Leonard told me on the telephone. There was a file protected by another password. It took him a long time but he found something about a woman called Concetta Gallo. Everything is in Italian. He asked for help to get it translated into English. Why did Cristina Martin use Holly's computer? Cristina Martin lives in New York, and Holly lived in Boston. Maybe the computer belonged to Cristina Martin and she gave it to Holly. Or Holly found it, or stole it, or bought it."

There was a knock at the door. Glenda went to the door and opened it.

A young woman was standing at the door holding a folder. "I'm Sherrie Botham," she said. "Captain Hollister told me to come and see you. I have some information about the Warburton family."

"That's great!" said Glenda. "Come in."

Sherrie sat down on Glenda's bed. She started to read from her notes.

"The Warburton family came here about ten years ago. They bought the house as soon as they arrived. They don't seem to have any friends. They don't talk to anyone. They don't belong to a local church or to any clubs. There is a son, Paul. He went to the local school for about three years. Then he stopped going to school. He has some big health problems. For the past few years he has been in a private hospital near Burlington in Vermont. He is eighteen years old now. His parents go to visit him three times a week. It is a very expensive hospital. Mr and Mrs Warburton must be very rich.

"I did a national search of births and found that the Warburtons had another child, a daughter, Holly Elizabeth. She was born in California. If she was still alive, she would be twenty now. But I guess she is the murdered girl.

"But this is strange. There is no record for her from schools or doctors or dentists in this area. It seems that she never lived in Plattsburgh!"

9. MR WARBURTON TELLS HIS STORY

Glenda thanked Sherrie. "You helped us a lot," she said. "Please thank Captain Hollister too. We will come to the police station soon."

Sherrie left and Jed said, "Lunch! I'm hungry!"

They walked to the diner across from the motel. It was now 2:00pm. The diner was almost empty and they sat at a table in a corner, where no one could hear them. They ordered hamburgers and coffee. After the waitress served their meals, Glenda took out a notebook.

"This is very strange. But maybe we can work it out," she said. She started writing notes.

"Mr and Mrs Warburton had two children. Holly was the older one. She was murdered in Boston. The younger child is Paul. He has been in a private hospital in Vermont for a long time. No one in Plattsburgh ever saw Holly. I think Sherrie is right. She never lived here. But when we went to the house, I asked to see Holly's bedroom. Mrs Warburton showed me a room for a young girl. She said they decorated it for Holly when she was nine. Why? Holly wasn't there. She never lived there."

Jed ate his hamburger and thought about it. "Often when children die, their parents keep the child's room just the way it was. I guess it is a kind of memory. Or maybe a way of pretending the child is still alive," he said. "Maybe when they came to Plattsburgh, they made that bedroom as a memorial for Holly."

"So Holly was already dead when they came to live here? That makes no sense," said Glenda.

"It makes sense, if the woman who was murdered in Boston wasn't Holly Warburton!" said Jed.

"But the Warburtons signed Holly's college entrance papers. Their address was on all the college records. It's a mystery," said Glenda rubbing her eyes. "I have a headache."

"The only person who can tell us the answer is Mr Warburton," said Jed. "I am going to call him. You have the phone number, don't you?"

Glenda gave Jed the telephone number and he made the call.

"Mr Warburton," he said. "This is Detective Jed Smith. My partner and I came to your house this morning. You have a lot of questions to answer. You must talk to us. You can go to the police station in Plattsburgh or you can come and meet us in the diner opposite the Good Value Motel on Catherine Street. If you say 'no', I am going to ask the local police to arrest you."

Jed listened and then said "OK. We'll see you in about fifteen minutes then."

He turned to Glenda. "Mr Warburton will come here."

Jed and Glenda ordered more coffee and waited. The diner was empty. Soon Mr Warburton arrived. He saw them and walked over to their quiet corner.

"Sit down, Mr Warburton," said Jed. "I think you have something to tell us."

Mr Warburton sat down and put his head in his hands. "I will tell you everything," he said quietly.

"I am a writer. I write romance novels. I use the name Elizabeth Hollywell because everyone thinks romance novels are written by women. Romance novels are more interesting if the action takes place in exciting locations.

"We lived in California, but I travelled to many parts of the world. My family always came with me. It was a great life. Eleven years ago we were staying in the mountains in northern Spain. We rented a tiny house in a village. It was a happy time. One day, my wife drove to a bigger town to buy food. Holly and Paul went with her. On the way back there was an accident. My wife drove the car off the road. It rolled down a hill and crashed. Amabel, my wife, and Paul were not badly hurt, but Holly died.

"It was terrible. My wife couldn't travel. So we had a funeral for

Holly in the little village. After the funeral, my wife became very depressed and ill. We went back to California, but my wife was so unhappy. Everything in the house, everything about our life, reminded her of Holly. She wouldn't let me tell anyone that Holly was dead. She wouldn't talk to anyone. She didn't want anyone to know that she was driving the car. She believed she killed Holly. It was her fault.

"So we moved here to Plattsburgh. I thought life would be better, but it wasn't. My wife made a bedroom for Holly. She copied everything from Holly's room in California. She thought Holly was still alive. She cooked Holly's favourite meals. She talked about her all the time.

"But little by little, my wife got better. Some days she didn't talk about Holly at all. Then Paul became very ill. Holly was dead. Paul is our only child. He will never get better, but we wanted to make his life as good as possible. We didn't have good medical insurance. Everything was very expensive. I borrowed money from the bank. I couldn't write any books. When I sat at my computer I couldn't think of anything. So I wasn't earning any money. I couldn't pay the money back to the bank.

"Then one day a young woman came to see me. She said she wanted to take the college entrance exams and go to college. She couldn't use her own name. She needed an identity. She wanted to use Holly's name. She knew that Holly had died In Spain. She knew that no one in America knew that Holly was dead. She knew that Paul was very ill, and we needed money.

"She wanted me to pretend that I was her father. She wanted to use our address here in Plattsburgh. First I said 'no'! But then she said she would pay me two million dollars. I thought it was a lot of money to pay to go to college. I guessed there was another reason. But Paul was so ill, and my wife was so unhappy.

"I love Paul and Amabel very much. Holly is dead. I thought, *The money will make life better for Paul. Holly loved Paul very much. She would want me to do this.* So I said 'yes'.

"The young woman sent me a bank cheque for two million dollars. I didn't have to do very much. Some letters came to the house and I sent them to a post office box in Rochester. She sent some papers to us, and Amabel and I signed them. Then, there was nothing. I never saw the young woman again. She never wrote to me or called. When more letters came I sent them to the same post office box. I knew she was in college in Boston, but that's all.

"We used the money to pay for Paul to stay in the private hospital. We never used any of the money for ourselves. After a while, I started writing again. I make enough money for Amabel and I to live on, but we could never pay the medical and hospital bills without the money I got from the young woman. Then I got the phone call to say that she was dead. It was a nightmare. I didn't know what to do. We didn't know her. I met her one time only, but everyone thought she was our daughter!"

Mr Warburton was crying now.

"That's all. I know I did a terrible thing but I didn't want to hurt anyone. I didn't want anything bad to happen. I thought she was a nice young woman."

Glenda thought it was a very sad story. "Mr Warburton. What was her name?"

"I don't know! She never told me! The money was a bank cheque. There was no name on it. The post office box name was King Company. I found a funeral company in Rochester. I sent them money to pay for the funeral and burial. I thought maybe I could do that. Maybe she has some family or something there. I don't know. But they won't know what name to use. She's not my daughter. She's not Holly!" Mr Warburton was shouting.

Jed went to the counter of the diner and asked for another cup of coffee. He brought it back and put it in front of Mr Warburton.

"Drink this. It will make you feel better," he said.

Mr Warburton drank thirstily and calmed down. He stopped crying.

"What will happen now?" he asked. "Will I go to prison? Will I have to give the money back? Amabel is not strong. Today she thinks Holly is still alive and nine years old! I have to look after my wife and son! What will happen to Amabel and Paul?"

"I don't know," said Glenda quietly. "I don't know what will happen. We will have to find out more about the money, and the young woman who died. I think you should go home and try not to worry too much. Someone will call you, or come to see you. But I don't know when."

Jed took Mr Warburton out of the diner. He waited until Mr Warburton drove away. Then he went back and sat down at the table with Glenda.

"What should we do now?" he asked.

"Well, we should call our boss in Boston and tell her the story. We should go and report to Captain Hollister. And then…" Glenda stopped talking.

"And then?" asked Jed.

"I think we should go to Rochester," answered Glenda.

10. ROCHESTER

Glenda called Mercedes Costa, their boss in the Boston Police Department. Mercedes agreed that they could go to Rochester.

"But come back to Boston right after that," she said. "I still have most of the staff away with colds and influenza. I need you back here."

They checked out of their motel, visited Captain Hollister and were soon on the way to Rochester. As Jed drove down the I87, Glenda talked about what they knew.

"The young woman who was murdered in Boston was not Holly Warburton. She had a lot of money. She had two types of clothes. Expensive business clothes and student clothes. When she died she was wearing the kind of dress women wear to a formal party. Her housemate did not know very much about her life. Her boyfriend didn't know much about her life either. She has some connection with Rochester because she told Mr Warburton to send the letters about college there. I think that her real name is Cristina Martin. "

"Why would a successful business woman want to be a student?" asked Jed.

"Mmm." Glenda opened her bag and took out a folder. She opened it and took out a piece of paper. "I have the doctor's report here. Remember he wrote that she was about thirty years old? I thought it was a mistake. But of course, a successful business woman would be more than twenty years old."

"I agree, but it still doesn't explain anything," answered Jed.

It was late when they got to Rochester, but the funeral company office was still open. "We have come to talk about the funeral for the young woman who was murdered in Boston," Glenda said to the woman at the main desk. She showed the woman her police badge.

The woman smiled. "Oh, yes. Holly Warburton. So sad. Such a young person. There is a private funeral arranged for tomorrow. It will be at the Parklands Garden cemetery at eleven am."

"Well. You can't have a funeral tomorrow," said Glenda. "The young woman is not Holly Warburton. You can't have a funeral until we know who she is."

The woman was surprised. She opened a file on her computer and looked at it.

"But we received instructions from a Mr Warburton in Plattsburgh. He said the young woman was his daughter, Holly Elizabeth. He said there were reasons why no one could come to the funeral. He asked us to make sure everything was as beautiful as possible. He sent money through the bank to pay for it all."

"We know that," said Jed. "But we have new information. Can you cancel everything until we know who she is?"

"We will have to," said the woman. "It is not convenient, but we can't have a funeral for someone with the wrong name or with no name! I must make some phone calls now."

"We'll be back tomorrow," said Jed. He walked towards the door but Glenda didn't move. "One more question," she said to the woman. "Has anyone else asked about the funeral arrangements?"

"Yes. I got a phone call asking where the funeral would be, and when. It was a man. He knew Mr Warburton's name, so I told him and he said thank you. He ended the telephone call before I could ask his name. Now I can't contact him to tell him there will be no funeral tomorrow."

Glenda and Jed found a small hotel nearby and checked in. Later, they met in the hotel lounge to discuss what they could do.

"I called Mercedes and told her what we found out," said Glenda. "She has copies of Leonard's emails about the files on the computer. She thinks the dead woman is probably Cristina Martin. She asked Leonard to look at everything again and to find out everything he could about Cristina Martin and her business. She told Pete to help Leonard. She wants some answers quickly."

Jed turned on his laptop. He looked at his emails.

"There is a new message from Leonard. It's a long one! Cristina

Martin closed her company more than two years ago. Then Cristina Martin disappeared. All the money from the business was transferred to a bank account in the name of Holly Warburton. But the two apartment buildings and the townhouse are still registered in the name of Cristina Martin. None of her business colleagues saw her or heard from her after that. Until three days ago."

"What happened?"

"Leonard found the names and addresses of all the companies in New York Cristina Martin did business with. Then Mercedes asked Pete to call all of them. The owner of a boutique told Pete that he had not seen or heard of Cristina Martin since she closed her company. Then three days ago, he was in Boston on a business trip. On Tuesday night, he was at the Restaurant Rosamunde. It's a very expensive restaurant, with some private dining rooms upstairs. He is sure he saw Cristina Martin get into an elevator. He guessed she was eating in one of the upstairs private rooms. Pete spoke to the restaurant owner and looked at the bookings for Tuesday night. Only one of the upstairs rooms was reserved on Tuesday night. A meal was served to two people. The reservation was in the name of John Smith.

"Pete also spoke to the waiters and kitchen staff. One of the diners was an old man, who seemed to be very ill. He arrived before the restaurant was open. He was in a wheelchair. He had two nurses with him. They took him up to the room and stayed with him until the other guest arrived. Then they went down and sat in an ambulance parked behind the restaurant."

"This is really interesting," said Glenda. "Can we call Leonard?"

"I guess he is still at work. He won't be happy, but I guess he will talk to you. What do you want to know?" asked Jed.

"If there are security cameras around the restaurant, then we could get the license number of the ambulance and find out who the man was. I am sure his name is not John Smith!"

Glenda called Leonard and asked him about the security cameras. While Leonard was talking, she made some notes. When she finished her call, she put her phone back on the table and smiled at Jed.

"Leonard is very good at his job. He already thought about the security cameras and found where the ambulance came from. It belongs to a private ambulance company here in Rochester! On Tuesday the ambulance driver picked up a man and two nurses from a house near here, and bought him back very early Wednesday morning," said Glenda.

"Do you have a name?" asked Jed.

"Of course! The name is Geno Gallo," answered Glenda.

"Shall we go now?" asked Jed.

"No. I don't think so," said Glenda slowly. "It seems he is an old and sick man. I think we should wait until tomorrow."

11. WHO IS HOLLY?

At nine o'clock the next morning, Glenda and Jed drove up to a large two-storey house, surrounded by a high metal fence. Jed stopped the car outside the security gates and Glenda got out. There was an intercom.

She pushed the button.

"Yes?" a voice came out of the speaker. "What do you want?"

"This is Detective Glenda Durek from the Boston Police Department. In the car is Detective Jedburgh Smith. We want to speak to Mr Geno Gallo."

"Wait," said the voice.

Glenda and Jed waited for about five minutes. Then, "He'll see you. Come to the main door."

The gates opened, Glenda got into the car and Jed drove along the driveway to the main entrance at the front of the house. A man was waiting for them there.

"Come this way," he said.

Jed and Glenda followed the man into the house and along a hallway. The man stopped at a double door, and opened it.

"Go in," he said.

Glenda and Jed entered a large, sunny room. On the far side of the room was a hospital bed. Two nurses were helping the man in the bed to sit up. Then they put two chairs by the side of the bed.

The man in the bed spoke. "Come over here."

Jed and Glenda walked over to the bed. "Mr Gallo?" asked Jed.

"Yes." The man turned to the nurses. "Go now. I'll call you when

I need you."

The nurses left the room and Glenda and Jed sat down.

"Thank you for seeing us," said Jed. "We have to ask you about Tuesday night. Were you in Boston that night?"

"Yes," said Mr Gallo. "I went down to Boston to see my daughter. It was her birthday."

"But Mr Gallo, you are very ill. Why didn't your daughter come to see you?" Glenda was puzzled.

"I didn't tell her I was ill. We hadn't met for a long time. She didn't know."

"And your daughter is Cristina Martin?"

"No. My daughter used that name for many years, but her real name was Concetta Gallo."

"And when she died, was she using the name Holly Warburton?" asked Jed.

"Yes. When she was murdered, she was using the identity of Holly Warburton," answered Mr Gallo.

"We are very sorry for your loss," said Glenda quietly. "We want to find her murderer. We hope you can help us."

"Water," said Mr Gallo. Jed got up and helped Mr Gallo to drink a little water. Then he helped him to rest back against the pillows.

"I will tell you the story of Geno Gallo, his daughter Concetta and why she died. I am not a good man. I have done many bad things in my life. In the beginning, in my hometown in Italy, I was not such a bad person. But I killed my best friend, Angelo. It was an accident, but no one believed me. His family were very powerful. They planned to kill me. I escaped to America. I joined a gang here. I became a lifetime criminal. I hurt people. I killed people. I made many enemies. My enemies wanted to kill me. My life became dangerous. Some of Angelo's family moved to America. They were looking for me. They also planned to kill me. So I had old enemies, and new enemies. They were powerful and clever. I had a lot of money but it was hard to enjoy life when so many people wanted to kill me. I went to Mexico and hid there. I met a young woman. Her name was Julietta. We fell in love. She was only twenty, and I was nearly fifty years old, but it was real love. She became pregnant. I wanted her to have the best care, the best doctors. We came back to the USA. Our daughter, Concetta, was born. We had a few months of perfect happiness, and then my enemies found us. They killed my wife. They shot her and left a message. The message said "…next your daughter, and then you…". I didn't care about myself. Since Julietta was dead, I wanted to die too. But there was Concetta. I had to live for her. I had to keep her safe."

Mr Gallo stopped talking. His face was grey. He looked terrible.

"Shall I call the nurse?" asked Glenda.

"No. No. I must tell you," answered Mr Gallo. He started talking again. His voice was very weak. It was hard to hear his words.

"I found a good Spanish family. Their family name was Martin. They took Concetta. They gave her a new name, Cristina. They took her away. She didn't know about her mother, Julietta, or me. It broke my heart. I could never see her, but the most important thing was that she was safe.

"I followed her life, so I always knew where she was and what she was doing. She studied languages. Started a business. She was a wonderful young woman. I was proud. I thought, *I have done one good thing in my life.*

"I stayed in hiding, but over the years my life became easier. My enemies died or went to prison. I was not in danger any more. I came here to live in Rochester. I started using my own name again. Then Concetta's Spanish parents died. I thought I could talk to my daughter. Almost three years ago, I contacted her. We met. She came to visit me here. It was difficult, but after a few months we developed a good relationship.

"Concetta was always travelling for her business, and I didn't want anyone to know her true story. So we didn't meet often. It was not perfect. There was too much sad history and I am not a good man. But it was enough for me.

"Then there was a disaster. The young man I killed in Italy had a brother. The brother came to the United States many years ago. His son and grandson were killed in Chicago. I don't know who killed them. I think it was a gang war. But the family remembered me. They thought I had killed them. The old enemies came back. They were hunting for me. Now Concetta was in danger again. A child was dead. They would try to kill my child before they killed me.

"I told Concetta she must hide. I told her she must change her identity. It was very difficult for her but she agreed. I told her she must change everything - her age, her lifestyle, her city. She closed her business, took a new identity and moved to Boston."

"How did you find out about Holly Warburton?" asked Jed.

"I didn't," said Mr Gallo. "Concetta did. She was buying fine leather in the mountains in Spain. She heard from the people in a small village about the American family and the daughter who died. They showed her Holly's grave.

"When she was looking for a new identity, she remembered the story. We checked. Holly's death was never recorded in America. She hired a detective to find the Warburtons. When she knew about the son's illness, it was easy. Concetta became a twenty-year-old student, called Holly Warburton.

"I stayed away from her, to keep her safe. I didn't call or message her, or write to her. But then I became ill. Last month, my doctors told me I only have a few more weeks to live. I wanted to see my daughter one last time. Tuesday was her birthday. I sent her the most beautiful dress I could find. It was a present for my princess.

"I wanted to say good bye and tell her I was sorry. I didn't go to her house. But I thought it would be safe to meet in a private room at a restaurant. Just one time.

"We had a wonderful evening. I was so happy. She was shocked when she saw me. I told her not to be sad. I said I would die soon, but then she would be free to have a good life. I was wrong. I am a selfish old man. I did what I wanted, and now she's dead.

"One of my enemies must have followed me from Rochester to Boston. After dinner, she rode in the ambulance with me. We went to her townhouse. To be careful, we didn't go to the front entrance. We stopped in the small street behind the townhouses. She said she would go in the back door. She kissed me. She got out of the ambulance, and we drove away.

"Then someone killed her."

"Did you see any cars in the street? Or any people?" asked Jed.

Mr Gallo smiled at him. "You can't see anything when you are lying flat on your back in an ambulance!"

"Sorry," said Jed. "That was a stupid question. Maybe one of the nurses, or the ambulance driver saw something."

Mr Gallo's face changed suddenly. He was having trouble breathing. Glenda was worried. She pushed the emergency bell and ran to the door. The nurses came running.

"Please leave," said one of the nurses. "He is very ill."

Glenda and Jed went outside and sat in the car.

"Did you believe Mr Gallo?" Jed asked Glenda.

"Oh, yes," said Glenda. "The story all makes sense now. Even the mystery file about someone called Concetta. I guess maybe Holly, no not Holly, not Cristina, Concetta! Concetta wanted to keep some record of her real identity."

"Do you think we will find out who killed her?" asked Jed.

"No," said Glenda. "Maybe we will be lucky and the ambulance driver will give us some useful information. But if it was a paid killer or a member of one of the gangs, it will be difficult."

Jed yawned and stretched. "I'm tired. Let's check out of the hotel and go back to Boston."

"I agree. We may never know who killed Concetta, but at least we found out who Holly was."

THANK YOU

Thank you for reading Who is Holly? (Word count: 11,730) We hope you enjoyed meeting our Boston detectives Jed and Glenda.

If you would like to read more graded readers, please visit our website http://www.italkyoutalk.com

Other Level 3 graded readers include
A Dangerous Weekend
A Holiday to Remember
Akiko and Amy Part 1
Akiko and Amy Part 2
Akiko and Amy Part 3
Be My Valentine
Different Seas
Enjoy Your Business Trip
Enjoy Your Homestay
I Need a Friend
Old Jack's Ghost Stories from England (1)
Old Jack's Ghost Stories from England (2)
Old Jack's Ghost Stories from Ireland
Old Jack's Ghost Stories from Japan
Old Jack's Ghost Stories from Scotland
Old Jack's Ghost Stories from Wales
Party Time!
Stories for Christmas

The Curse
Together Again

ABOUT THE AUTHOR

I Talk You Talk Press is a Japan-based publisher of language textbooks, graded readers and language learning/teaching resources.

Our team is made up of highly experienced language teachers and translators, who have all studied at least one additional language to an advanced level.

This experience enables us to design our materials from the perspective of both the teacher and the learner. We consult with both teachers and language learners when designing our textbooks and graded readers, and test our materials extensively in the classroom before publication.

We are a fast-growing press, and currently publish graded readers for learners of English. We publish new graded readers monthly.

www.ingramcontent.com/pod-product-compliance
Lightning Source LLC
Chambersburg PA
CBHW022347040426
42449CB00006B/751